Karac   ing

For Jasmin, my luck

Karaoke King

Dai George

Seren is the book imprint of
Poetry Wales Press Ltd.
Suite 6, 4 Derwen Road, Bridgend, Wales, CF31 1LH
www.serenbooks.com
facebook.com/SerenBooks
twitter@SerenBooks

The right of Dai George to be identified as
the author of this work has been asserted in accordance
with the Copyright, Designs and Patents Act, 1988.

ISBN: 978-1-78172-628-0
ebook: 978-1-78172-629-7

A CIP record for this title is available from the British Library.

The publisher acknowledges the financial assistance of the Books Council of Wales.

Cover artwork: James Donovan
jamesdonovanart.com

Printed in Bembo by Severn, Gloucester.

Contents

I

Doxology	9
Aisles	10
Poem on 27th Birthday	12
The Park in the Afternoon	15
Fooled Evening	16
Cooking with Butter	17
God Willing	18
Universal Access	20
Far Enough Away	21
Rock vs Pop	22
Dustin Hoffman in Biarritz	23
Real Rain	24
Station to Station	25
Valet	26
The Disclaimer Room	27
Agoraphobia	28
Near Historical Swoon	29
Karaoke King	30
Neck of the Chicken	31
Contact Again	33
Ubi Caritas	34

II
from A History of Jamaican Music

Referendum Calypso	37
Or, a Prelude	39
Bus to Skaville	40
People Rocksteady	41
Knows It, Scratch	42
The Night (Dub)	43
Or, a Windrush Interlude	44
Soon Forward	45
Toasting for Pronouns	48
Party Time	49

III

September's Child   53
Wards   54
Post-Historical Teatime   55
American Gratitude   56
New York Morning, Six Years On   58
Sun Has Spoken   60
Poem in which my hairline recedes   61
Shopping with Mam   62
Obsolete Heartbreak Suite   63
Doggies   64
Benevolence Test   65
The Mercury Mine   68
Pink Cones   69

Notes and Acknowledgements   70

I

We are close enough to childhood, so easily purged
of whatever we thought we were to be.

Robert Duncan, 'Food for Fire, Food for Thought'

Doxology

Blessings flow, through narrow fields, a weir
            finds restitution as it falls.
       Tightroping gulls, the crumbling edge
is anxious as they slip and cling to show them
          peace below. I number the blessings
in a split and democratic sky.
        The clemency of inland water.
The resourcefulness of creatures left to try.

Blessings flow, but trouble finds me
in the impasse after rain. I mean democratic
        as an argument that neither side can win.
Praise grass from which the pylons ship
        invisible cargos that I wait upon
unthinkingly, an emperor inured to the hand
        that serves him fruit.

You'll find little god here but demanding
        drifts of pollen, little trouble but a boy
whose dream last night was of a concert
        and his frozen voice.
       The gulls find trouble in a moment
they can't trust, a wind that smashes them aloft

then drops beyond the river.
                    Obstacles and carrion,
      fluidity and rest, a hatchling woken
in its nest of foil.   The parliament still warring
       through its agonies of choice,
the hustle never ending
          nor the trouble   nor the joy.

Aisles

Plenitude and frigid air: death
could never come where fruit
will never rot before it's sold
or thrown away. I could never be
mistreated, never fall to mischief
in this humming galleon of service
down whose many-jarred and many-
branded gangways I could trip
forever, never sickening or asking
where it comes from, how. Bacon
sweats beneath its plastic corset.
On empty schoolnights we
would drive here, newly licensed,
and plunder the golden sundries
of the deli counter, less in hunger
than enchanted boredom: bhajee, satay
skewer, olive bar, layered salad
reduced to clear, the decadent
barbarian empire of freezers and
lurid condiments, beyond which lay
the household aisles, our lives
mapped out by ergonomic grid.

I lied when I said I never
wonder how it happens; how
like a quietly ovulating mammal
these shelves replenish. It speaks
of a greater kindness working
in our world than I'd assumed.
A providence less radical and more
assured. It stuns me into apathy
the colour and thin consistency
of milk expressed and pasteurised
by exploited farmers. Returning
here alone this frightened evening,
I knelt down among the chicken
strips and mince, dreaming myself
a worm in the field that reared

such miracle and blight. I've never
known a hunger worse than two
pounds in my pocket here could quell.
My anger may never meet the air
but lies in wait, flesh under wax
in fruit that's yet to perish, or to sell.

Poem on 27th Birthday

The osteria's blasting jazz, the slick and fruity
after-hours sort, while down the street a Fiat stereo
fronts up with a folksy Anglophonic strum.
I'm down with it all; I'm a honey trap for wasps
snuffling the grains in my espresso cup,
but those bastards don't bug me any more. No,
the dread in this young daddio's soul derives
mainly from the monoglotic cringe that comes
in proffering twenty *per un grande bicchiere*
and hearing, 'Do you have any smaller change?'

It's hard to start again. On the way here,
a sculpture of two people kissing was less
a weight of metal that stuck in my chest
and more…

I know this Fiat song – I heard it first
one Friday night at home with a talent show,
where the person singing it reached out, aching,
and her mentor boogied in the aisles.

Today is a first bite of well-hung steak,
the middle third commencing in a long life's
lunch. I chowed down the starters in a haze
but today is marbled and glossy and rare.

Two tables across, a group of girls
could be fifteen or twenty, happy or stuck,
with a baby mauling the sides of his pram
and the red-capped dad, or likely dad,
lipping a roll-up, thumbing his phone.

A sculpture of two people kissing should dare
a timid heart to back itself, and I
should know the name of this song,
this warbly, flighty, homely strum,

just as a jazz cat should know when to stop,
and a wasp should be smooth to the rump, and my luck
should be turning, not turning the world on its head,
and a boy should feel lucky he's drinking, not dead,
or at least that he's watching impossible wars
play out on the TVs of hill-town bars
on a boot-shaped peninsula, not one where drones
patrol the residential blocks.

My luck is fine. You're my luck. I'm working
through the end of luck, and today,
though far from me, you're still the sculpture
flexing into flesh and breath.

No, the guy's not the dad, any more than
the venerable pair on the suntrap bench
are married, or kin to the gurgling kid,
for all that they'll pop over now and check
if the mama's helping him grow up strong,
if the guy's got a light, if he saw what went on
at Juve this Sunday, and – *I belong to you* –
I'm digging the hell outta this Fiat jam,
for all that it makes the noodly hum
behind me sound like the *Rites of Spring*.

In younger days, when opinions were crisp,
astringent as radicchio, I'd have declared myself
immune to its sickly charms, to anything
sunnyside-up and blancmange, so lacking
in phobia, friction, demands, but – *You belong to me* –
it floats to me now as nothing less
than the Glory of Love. The old boy raps
pink sports pages on the tabletop.
Cuore Kaka. Milan è casa mia.
His young friend shrugs and arranges his cap
in an opposite sideways angle and laughs.

Today's been flashed on the griddle and served.

The osteria flips the disc. Teddy Pendergrass
gets jiggy all over his chorus line. Kaka's
come home. Ain't no stopping us now,
and as the Fiat down the street affirms
you're my sweetheart. What a mute wonder
love is. It's here, it's the bench, it's the statue
and a dog, loping where the old boy goes
when the sun sends him in for a kip.

Ain't no stopping us, sweetheart, though only now
do I hear the modesty in the boast. The calm.
It means no more than we'll get to the next.
Summer here has one month left in pomp.
Halfway down my second beer, this wasp
grazed my knuckle and I didn't flinch.

The Park in the Afternoon

By the goats, a high-vis warden
tweezers litter with glacial care.
Men bear tins of Scrumpy Jack aloft
to salute Ol' Blue Eyes as he spreads
the news from a battered tape machine.
Their conductor lies down in the grass
crafting languorous signals from a spliff.

On the lunchtime news, a minister
reviled my productivity:
sleepwalking into a crisis
is how he described the nation's plight
when output fails to tack with growth.
Watching a duckling wobble afloat
as sun glints, useless, on the pond,

I see his point. Diverse and splendid
things have brought us here, we heathens
in the Christendom to come. The drunk,
the retired, the roistering lads
bunking off early with blazer sleeves
riding up their arms – each of us
truant, and gentle for an hour,

our output no more than
what we can make
of the angle of
hurried daylight before
a shower.

Fooled Evening

This weather's been a ruined party now for years.
It mugs and flatters, grinding through its old
routine while drifting out of key.

It's warmer now, but sicklier and wearied.
The crime unfolded by degrees, starting with
a skipped summer, a year when it never quite
came together, as if summers per se were too
much an effort, too crass an ensemble of salt
sea and pollinated air, and the weather simply
wanted out. It was the embarrassment

of finding out too late: were that cringe a colour,
it would manifest tonight, in a sky that stays up
past its tucking in. You want to name it after oily fish,
but mottling won't capture the ubiquity and gaucheness
of this light. Leaves fret stupidly on branches
long after the hour change, yet evening comes
and keeps on coming, straining always later
to be seen. It's like nobody told it how
we dress these days, how deep run our austerities.
It peacocks to solstice, with the unmerited
confidence of a baby boom – a onetime dandy
overdressing, after the fashion has changed.

Cooking with Butter

for the unction of arborio
for ecological disaster will devour me in time
for the puritan in me has a nagging mouth, and I must stuff it with gold
for by butter's foam I've known the spread of offshore wealth
for the fish adheres to it
for the acupuncture of butter on fish's skin
for the erotics of my death and the mortification of my sex
for the hand slips, as with salt or gin

for my parents renounce it with the venial sins
for the state is weak and money strong
for mushrooms bloat with it and render flavour
for the cow knows more than I know what I want
for an omelette is important, its softness to be nurtured
for the grave will give my protein in return

God Willing

Your coat fits now, if only bulked-out for the funeral
with a suit bought for the occasion off-the-peg. I shrug
   my shoulders in the pads and think of you
         in Oxford for the day before your first big job,
    submitting to a tailor eking tape
      across your chest. His accent frightens you.
It sounds like it should belong
       to someone off the wireless reporting on a bomb
  that's levelled half of London in a stroke.
        It seems to question
whether every penny in the cheque you've scrawled will clear
      and honestly you share his doubts. You know that nothing's
  safe until you hold it in your hand,
    a lesson bludgeoned home
  with trapdoor force when twelve years old
    you heard the news a train
           had killed your father as he worked the line
    and left you
        everything:
      the wit to fix a skirting board,
  to wrestle sacks of coal,
     to kiss your mother
as she moaned at you and wept.

From that day on you never promised
    so much as prayed: *God willing*, meaning chance
        of rain, *God willing*, meaning come to me again
   when money can be relied on
  like a boiler beneath the stairs. I hated it,
    that hesitance,
        your tilted head – the love
  that couldn't bear to disappoint
   so beat back hope instead. It's only now
      you've died

and left me promiseless
I try it on my tongue. It tastes
    of paraffin and rationed meat,
        of varnished chapel halls. It chokes me as I try
                                to make it stick –
the glue of it dissolves. *God willing* I'll leave tailoring behind.
            God willing there'll be anyone
        to sign for it and mourn. In the sunlit crematorium
    an organ faintly drones. You wait for us
        to reach you, foursquare
                    to the end, and yet
        I cry to find your bones so light
                            and speechless as I hoist
your coffin on my shoulders, in the coat you bought to last.

Universal Access

I have only ever lived among pollution. Tell me it is not the sky I look at but an irradiated blanket, pitched between my streetlamps and the real sky. To that I say the real sky is immaterial, an idea cast too far back into the dark to matter. My pollutions define me.

As a child I favoured invented worlds, populated by tribes with kaleidoscopic cultures, another one always over the mountain ridge. Today, in the city, the promise of a never spent or perfected flux is all that keeps me here. The new thing ever opening. Frontiers of the affordable and good.

I am stranded in the middle of *Moby Dick*: p.274 out of 509. The Pequod, after listing in the South Pacific, has embarked upon its first 'cutting in', the process of safely flaying a whale of its blubber, which requires the whole crew to heave a hook-fed rope through the blowhole until everything gives at once, for *the blubber envelopes the whale precisely as the rind does an orange.*

Part of me would sooner stay here. There is too much to read. Far from a complaint, this is only to state the necessary obverse of infinity's appeal. Were we to know that our present book was the last we were yet to read, its conclusion would be intolerable. Heaven, then, must be to choose a fixed point, knowing the brawl of infinite, receding options, as if slipping into a particular chair while rain hammers on the skylight. Here I can dip my fingers in the dripping hide.

Through my browser I watch a documentary, free of charge, about a church repurposed as a data centre where a record of every web page is collected through time. Truly, there is a holiness in this: shades of God's forensic love for hair and sand. As well as sites they preserve books scanned by human hand, so that Melville's relishing and fretful bulk can expand along its ultimate democratic tangent to take its place beside the novel's Wiki page, as captured on almost every day of its existence.

A great wall: a cliff face of servers cooled by fans. Several-coloured diodes blink in response to uploads, downloads, the servers that need replacing. In this hygienic temple, across a medium of distance and physical substance I will never understand, they are polluting me. It is dizzying, exquisite. My white whale plunges forever out of view. This is the structure of the new sky.

Far Enough Away

You mistake me for flesh: for the honest captain
who can follow where the cruising stars have signalled,
glittering and keen. My body isn't like that.
It remembers water, remembers it too well
when you come near, but returns each night
to settled pastures, indentured groves, the landlocked
love that doesn't think to guard or name its territories.

The mistake, I know, was mine, that I exhumed
this flesh suit in a mingling room and stood
surprised to find a real blood repopulate its limbs.
Will you sail with me? No, I wouldn't want that,
wouldn't want the queasy belly-sweetness as we left
that dock behind. You find me a bad and dusty ragdoll
dissembling on the quarterdeck, when my better flesh

is safe at home. The stars there are fixed and white as pills,
and I find them to my liking. I went back on myself today
to trace them, over fields of celibate frost and winter mud,
but even then, in the heart of my drowsy parklands,
far enough away from any salt or murky scent,
I happened on a weir carrying the din of water
from its mountain source towards a howling sea.

Rock vs Pop

for Roddy Lumsden

I've given up. Where would *Sister Lovers* sit?
When I first sniffed you out as kindred
in the promising bit of youth, I cared
to learn the verdict. Nowadays that quarrel
ranks with physics and virginity, as one
more thing I'm pleased I'll never have
to do again. Your answer was always
that it made no sense, to someone like you
who cribbed his brother's wax, through
the strange third of the '70s when glam,
pub and prog were the dough enveloping
a gooey custard heart of dross.

Punk happened in the metropolis,
to wilder girls and blades in scripted
threads, though magpies like you and me
know the moment of thieving and assemblage
belongs to anyone, at any time, regardless
of the flock. But I'm tired, fellow cutpurse,
I'm debating how to move. Once I had
the time and legs for both. I decked my hips
with flowers and I danced.

Alex Chilton keeps me company tonight,
snivelling like heaven at the witching hour.
At nighttime I go out and see the people…
Sung as if the night has never taken him
much farther than his chamber window
at an alpine sanatorium. I hope he recovers.
I hope he finds his shoes and makes
the journey he's been planning
with a friend who'll see him safe
and hold his case along the way.

Dustin Hoffman in Biarritz

The great roles having gone the way of the great mid-century
consensus, having frittered to a blob of fancy art-house shit,
he finds himself listing westward, skirting the Côte D'Azur,
abandoning his yacht at Perpignan and setting out in scuffed
designer espadrilles in search of exile, through Pyrenean foothills,
to a lesser bay whose waves froth white with gnarly rips.

His sadness is crippling, flamboyant yet exact. New Hollywood
never said this dotage would come his way, such carousel
of hackwork and lecherous decline. Beneath his leather tan
the flesh is latent, soft, though blood increasingly betrays a sense
of clotting wax, the dummy of his stardom setting inside-out.
His sadness casts a shadow farther than the presidential suite.
Who else was promised Mrs Robinson? On this windy coast
the daintiest dish holds back a barbarous smack of garlic.
They dig rugby like 5-star brutes, braying nasal Biscay vowels
along the esplanade. Who the hell even surfs anymore? In his casino-
hotel lobby, assuming the lotus position for the final time, he weeps
at being finally so apropos, so blank, so irretrievably lost, he laughs.

Real Rain

Deadbeat hangdog trudging on a bedroom wall
three-quarter-length in monochrome, a manchild
needing girl. Walking too long forever through
the filthy night, or idling outside the very
sickness he desires. Ambient porno makes
valiant hangdog puke. Hand-in-pocket incel
seeking girl to chaperone. Idling and seething
while the normies flirt and cum. They blank him
like they owe him more than freedom to be alone.

Real rain's what he wants, because real is what
never wins. Real is everything he has to give
and everything that's spurned. Everything
that hurts him isn't real. Married girls and
hookers fake and squeal. Antihero dreaming
of protection he can grant, favours only
he bestows, in the kingdom of his want.

Someday it's gonna drench them – some day
only he controls. In his vindicated heaven
they'll be first against the wall. Histrionic
mohawk turning water into blood, mounting
teenage bedrooms with his automatic gun.
He wants to know who's talking through
the silence he'd enforce. He wants to know
what's funny in a mutilated corpse. Patron saint
of fragile, nursing dreams of real men – dreams
of being washed out to the gutter with the scum.

Station to Station

after Bowie

Thin boys crash in second class, all memory
of how they got there fried. The journey is
a midnight trawl through morning's bluish
certainties. The thin boy is far from certain;
he has a gift in neglect, mysterious injuries,
a long way to go across a hostile continent.

White boys gather plaudits for their funk.
Their boogie is a ripe banana splitting
to sweet mush in your mouth. Relax,
or don't, for white boys can do opera;
their high notes scale a peak of need
then slum it, parley, get on down.

The Duke, though – the Duke repels
the waiting crowd with his half salute.
He forgot where he was. He slicks
his hair to Hollywood and smiles;
invites you to a séance in the louche
Grand Duchy of his personal hell.

Valet

I remember pleasure. He was
never the rake with a gaudy rose

poking from his buttonhole
but the silent, unassuming boy

who took my coat and let me pass
unencumbered to the many rooms

beyond his station. I looked for him today
in the clubhouse that he used to tend.

I searched in panic, door to door,
finding crews of plump and leisured men

who said, *Pour yourself a drink and sit.*
I tried. I stretched. But clad in wool

and weighed with it, I couldn't reach
the shelf that held their stout carafes.

The card games and the laughter
all went on without me, and my coat

stayed buttoned to the top.
My arms were heavy. I was very hot.

The Disclaimer Room

is very small. Smaller than you,
in fact, with its doorframes and
ceilings built an inch too short,
as if in a Tudor cottage where
the need to duck exemplifies
a gulf in time, a change in diet
or in labour. But there isn't any
double here, no ghost in a
soiled jerkin, harbouring
vicious beliefs about witches –

only you, bent over in a vest,
alone with your vulgarity and
waxy hair, the blank municipal
walls. There's a lot of filing left
to do but you feel frozen at
the cusp of it, choking on doughy
caveats: *I was young and poorly
advised, just repeating what I'd heard,
we went back and tidied up after,
I'd explain if only I could –*

Listen to yourself. The bar
full of jolly characters is gone,
all the uncles who meant no
harm. Now, get down to the
dogged grub work, settling
accounts to no one's credit.
Confess, by all means, to
whoever's there to hear it.
Mind you don't hit your head.

Agoraphobia

Wrongly, I suppose, the air
is hesitant and thick. Vacancy
surrounds me though the street
remains the same. The year is
much too open, or the carriage
not quite friendly, with an aspect
of written warning, as though
the city square had emptied.
But quieter than that. January
peeling leaf by foggy leaf to
other days the calendar won't
pardon. Virulent blue mornings,
with the birds a hostile chorus,
a walk in public to the forum
turning perilous then silent.
A summer goes flavourless
in my mouth or summer takes
on just the briny taste of fear
until I can't pretend to hold
myself or wake. Heaviness
unlifting. Brittle light. I try
to charm down flecks of neon
from the ceiling above my bed
but they're trapped behind my
eyelids, filaments burning grey.
It isn't me, then, but a stranger
who finally steps downstairs
and crosses over to a shop
that lets him in the door, a
jingle as he enters. No one
stares. Biscuits, toiletries,
tomatoes, cartoon treasure
of the sweet shelf, and he
buys it, I can buy it, using
money made of plastic, a
card that is accepted, just
a smile and no one cares.

Near Historical Swoon

Rotten lily, swollen tide: the smell, the shape, the guttering light
of years I held so cheap for seeming close. This near past, this absence
equal to desire: how I would clutch its bulk to me and breathe its musk
and shiver, could I only trap it, only trace its smoking spore.

Whole years that danced and fled before me, leaving less
to know them by than childhood hours, long days which
have mantled now, becoming history, their protagonist as fixed
and partly known as Caesar's wars. If nostalgia cuddles and provides,

it can't be that. This is visitation from the lost land close behind,
the space vacated every time I take my step. Uncanny valley,
whose inhabitants are awkward cousins to our present selves:
its laws and languages, the broadcasts on its radio resemble ours

except in all the minor ways they don't. I hear the dying bars
of a summer anthem from five years ago. Protests in the central square
of the capital city of a bad regime with whom we dealt in arms
and will again: less than a memory, the spectral flavour of it

catches in my throat. Street food, candle wax and sleeping bag.
To meet again the hope you thought was gone, which events
as they unfolded overtook. I was never there. Watching from afar,
I thought that spring would hold, and save me from the man

I was: a homebound drifter shuffling laps around the park,
his government embroiled in vested sleaze, all hopes for what
he'd come to be not far removed from what would pass,
but far enough the deficit will make him swoon.

Karaoke King

Mewl of a cat. The glass collector weeps.
Myfanwy staggers to her station by the till
beneath the gin. Abandon hope all ye who loiter
dithering at the door: my song won't tickle cockles
or make yr roundup of the year. Iambic so I am,
real dolorous and rusty, and my chanson
brings the house down to an empty bar.

Lovingly I swing the mic, an anxiety under
the influence, a gull who'd be the Sundance Kid,
descanting on his theme. Requests? I've killed
a few. The party never stopped. The Ponderosa
shook all night, while yr da was still in shorts.
Lilacs in springtime, hotdogs for tea, Blind Willie
Johnson's got nothin' on me. Huh. Like you care.

Coming this late in the night, my song demands a setting
like the fatal climax of a Sunday film. I'm trigger-hot
and rhinestoned with ancestral muck; I hear ghosts
marauding in the vault, whining at my back. Bless me,
fathers, for I have sneezed on the Wurlitzer. You'll
have to back me up here if my lover wakes. *Paham
mae dicter, o Myfanwy, yn llenwi'th lygaid duon di?*

She's stirring and I sense the swelling; the toxic male
voice pageant blossoms in the wings. Here they are,
the ruddy legends – all yr butties dressed in tuxes on the
pitchside of yr dreams. Belting out unchappelled hymns
with boiled-ham patriotic breath, their brigadier goat.
Bethesda and Moriah, I have known thy deacons! I lay
down beneath their corrugated roofs and raged

raged raged against the dying of the greener grass.
But the night is tapering, the taps are running low,
and Wales is nowhere nearer fathoming its pain.
Hey nonny no yippy yo yippy yay Hieronymo
can't be mad again. They flee from me who
lately made my sweet birds cheep. The ruined
choir goes brawling down the street.

Neck of the Chicken

Nan in pomp, regnant in her
electronic chair, cataloguing
hard things that have happened
to other people. 'Back when
your Bampy's father died…'

The coffee is milky and microwave-
hot; her memory like water. 'See,
after that she never wanted any-
one. People asked if she'd take
a man and she said *not if his arse*

came dripping in diamonds!' Laughter
breaks over the robotic whirr
as she toggles and her purple-
dappled legs are levered two
feet off the ground. 'Still,

I know what she meant by that
now.' She brushes cake crumbs
off the chair and glances side-
ways, measuring the space
where the other one used to be.

In the garden, chaffinches
and empty lawn – the glasshouse
catching dabs of sun. Autumn
outside is a light that wants putting
on in here, and I can't keep track

as she picks up ten years later
with Thatcher in Number 10.
I crawl into the childhood dark
of the den I made on visits here,
into the guts of the massive pine tree

she had cut down the same year
Bamps died. She wasn't getting
the benefit any more. 'One thing
you'd have to say is he always
got the neck of the chicken…'

She's talking now about someone
else, a friend from chapel or
Cwmbran – someone who grafted
but never settled, before keeling over
while he cleaned his teeth. Heart

attack, and he was thin as
an edge, with his mother
downstairs eating breakfast, too.
'It's a cruel world, Nan,' I say,
but it's more than that. It's

the interest of it, the occasional
serendipity. The flood that cancels
your honeymoon, then sweeps
off the hotel. With a pacemaker
the man survived, as people

sometimes do. Simultaneously
our attention drifts back to
the garden, where a squirrel
is going manic, trying to crack
open the compost bin. Nan tuts,

laughs, heaves herself afoot, missing
the moment the lock is sprung and
a week's worth of peel and teabags
topples loose. 'I wonder who'll
have it all when I'm gone. You

pile up some rubbish in a life-
time, see.' Her hand looms at the
mantelpiece, the shelves – the lawn
where a creature is racing home
with gristle in its mouth.

Contact Again

You needed your sleep so I let you,
collapsed against me like a bag
which may or may not have held
an incendiary device. Snoozing

stranger, while the night bus filled
and you tossed and turned to find
the meat between my shoulder
and my neck, I was a tingling

grid, my dormant nerves
fizzing to your presumption,
as when a tongue first wriggled over mine
in a kiss embarked on for a dare

or lately at a new salon
when after the cut I was led
to a marble basin and my head
was lowered in the groove.

Her massage worked up from
the base, consent far less solicited
than given, and scarcely knowing
what to do, I thanked her

as tonight I thanked your straying
beard, for reminding me that touch
is only touch when skin arrives
at knowledge that it didn't have before.

Ubi Caritas

also love   which is never one thing   but another
a star jump   redirecting blood   that silted through
the morning   the pattern of fear   unstitching
a desk or bed   that trapped you   in the logic
of its stillness   until love   not only tender love
but care   became the prompting   a synapse
opens   wind resumes   suspension trembles
underfoot   a bridge will   carry you over
it wasn't stillness   but a kind of death
that held you through the morning   why
did you wait all morning   at what risk
you can't become an absence   people mourn
a tree commemorating   tender love   a tree
grown too symbolic   or a bench   now the river
makes its case to you   the river angling   refreshing
how love   is only movement   and exchange
a care for the   becoming   how other things
will carry you   the river's saying *next*

II

from A History of Jamaican Music

I'm going home
with joy in my heart...

Errol Dunkley

Referendum Calypso

Songwriters will understand – the void
    before a melody arrives, when breath
can't seem to shape it. For a moment
the frets are all used up.
The merry-go-round creaks and whines.

This writer's twanging his guitar
    in an alley off the quayside
where he busks his wage. Same old
        yankee-doodle jive. Same
old rickety street-corner beat,
    a rhumba box on bass.

In come the crates of wheat
  and oil, acetates tucked
        in suitcase nooks
the dockers flog at interest.
    Already scratched, they wobble
on the deck, when he gets them home
      to learn the parts.

In this moment the song sounds tired
        and cold, on a thick-hot day
    Chicago or Philly can't rise to meet.

           Bauxite in the north,
heavy industry cuckooing the white suits
    on their slick resorts.
Sometimes he has half a mind
  to pitch up there and dig
    a month or two on union rates
      singing on break
till a lunchtime he gets a shoulder tap
    and an invitation to come down-coast
  to Ocho Rios, for bowtie-scatting
      and Day-O smiles, a boater
    passed around for tips.

He's breathing, and pursing, but the shape
won't come.

A referendum's in the air
and he's weighing
his vote. Some bonehead argument
about island rights, two parties
touting freedom as their aim
pounding your doorstep, hollering blood.
How d'ya like your independence served?
Bustamante on the radio: *a federation*
of paupers, foisted on us by Britain
to escape her ancient responsibilities…

He spits
on a cloth
and cleans
the bridge.

On the music station
they're playing a song
almost as a poll, or clock, on the hour.
It's got swing and heat, a sneer
in its grin, and it sounds like
it's finding a way.
Lord Laro and his players
calling out freedom over tumbling
pans, a song you could sip a cocktail to
till the fruit starts to turn in your glass.

Yes, yes, yes, federation, yes!
He picks out the E and shapes
an A. *No, no, no, federation, no!*
There's a dance
later on he's been meaning to check
but the moment's now for writing –
for playing along to Laro, finding space
between the grooves. He jags
against the downbeat
and it's *on.*

Or, a Prelude

'In an environment where any emerging indigenous – i.e., black – artistic or social expression was either discouraged to the point of being stillborn, drastically diluted in the name of artistic sophistication or blanded-out to appeal to white tourists, the sound system had been created by and for Jamaica's dispossessed. Thus it would always thrive so long as it remained their exclusive property. To reiterate Derrick Harriott's point, there was a huge sense of self-worth involved here: a warm night inside a big lawn's bamboo fence (clubs were so named because most of the action happened on the grassed-over area outside the actual hall), under the starry Caribbean skies, was about as good as life – anybody's life – could get. When the sweet smells of jerk chicken, bougainvillaea and collie weed swirled around your head, you could feel the hottest R&B jump-up vibrate through a cold bottle of beer, and cut some steps with a big-eyed daughter... it was enough to overwhelm anybody. To the point at which it didn't really matter what you didn't have for the rest of the time, because right there, right then, at the sound-system dance, you had it all.'[1]

Which is where

                                   I first come

     in

                       feeling *dispossessed* somehow

         at 18

                       wanting those sweet smells   starry skies

and a cold vibrating bottle

          to the point at which it

               doesn't matter

                     that I didn't catch the first bit

     about property   and in any case

        I tell myself

        didn't he say *anybody*

1. Lloyd Bradley, from *Bass Culture: When Reggae Was King* (London: Penguin, 2000).

Bus to Skaville

An idiot weekend, balanced on my boyhood's edge
like a pint of squash atop a mantelpiece.
A northbound 23 from town. Mid May
evening, and the bluebird scarves have flown
to roost in closets for the cricket months.

An aftershaved Malvolio, my quiff
yearning for action and pert with gel, I sit
on the empty, step-high upper deck and nurse
a bootless thought for Ellie Glynn, who may
or likely won't be at the gathering

I'm bound for. The lower level's Dai caps, canes,
shopping for the week and summer coats. I hoist
my earbuds home and blot it out. I'm sick of it –
it could be anything. Till now all songs have jangled
through the unrequited treble, so when

I switch the disc on Pantmawr Road
and my latest buy – a burgundy box
sporting a horse with a Trojan plume –
goes chick-a-boom and canters through my mind
as if the cover pic were being whipped

a heat comes down; a newly gifted knack
for walking with a naughty strut, and now
this pulse has quickened me I can't
be satisfied with reaching out
for Ellie Glynn's still-absent lips

or bobbing in my chartered hometown sea
which as of now has opened out
to ocean, and I won't be coming back
or answering to its clapped-out beat
for anything less than the Guns of Navarone.

People Rocksteady

Better get ready girl, your boy
is coming and he's learned the way
to syncopate and shake his head –
he isn't saying no. Though born
a loser, he scrubs up fine – his
steps have cooled to gladness.
He's at your door, a polo-shirt groom.
He's asking you down to the beach.

Hear the call girl, take his hand, shake
your shoulders, everything is fine.
Your conversation needn't rush. He's
learned, just as he worked to learn
these steps. His scent has mellowed
to a dab of something plain and fresh,
and soon you'll talk of simple things
that come out right, the breakers lapping

blue on white, so girl – could you
refuse? There's your brothers and sisters,
Uncle Freddie and all your friends,
and every song you'll hear tonight's
a hit, not in some other world
but this, where love is not a gamble
but your surest bet, a spearmint kiss
snatched in front of the rocking dance.

Knows It, Scratch

My grandmother dead, my poor heart spurned, the summer
slack with mourning, my sanctuary a café stove
where my father isn't crying. Handblender roar
and rarebit grease. Butter-singe of toastie smokes my shirts.

In the kitchen, radio swills and soothes
like dishwater lapping milky at my wrists.
Tip jar fattens with cash to blow
in Spillers, just a hop-skip over the arcade,

where education awaits in cardboard sleeves.
Today this gutless summer broke into a rash,
into an acne bloom of city heat. Bin bags poach
in alleys next to pubs leaked gaily down the Hayes

but Spillers keeps its classroom cool
and my choice today is *Super Ape*
bartered for a jewel case adorned
with King Kong roaring down the jungle.

He spurs me home through basking crowds,
the Taff banks strewn with lovers.
He helps me swerve my father's orphaned eyes
and rush upstairs where he can play.

Womp. Smoke. Galactic gorilla groove.
Trilling flute on nuclear bass. The day's
heat paddled by fans from wall to wall.
Grief baked heavy in my attic room.

I shed my stinking clothes and sit
in judgement, under thunder-swollen skies.
Who feels it knows it, yuh, Prince Jazzbo says.
Well, I feel it, Scratch. You know?

The Night (Dub)

You dipped your toe. You let your ankle break
the surface of a lake too deep and cold
to fathom, though a light

which seemed the moon reflected
beckoned you to enter to your waist.

Nicodemus came to Jah Jah by night
To ask him the way of salvation and right

This cold is wild, impatient,
careless of your birthrights. Breath
shrivels in it; your meandering thoughts

all clench and turn to muscle
or would do if you could let them,
if you could slip below the waterline.

O who will tell me where
He found thee at that dead and silent hour?

Darkness falls, a deep
and dazzling calm. You sink
two feet and open up your lungs.

You've got to be born again
You've got to be born again

Or, a Windrush Interlude

'As an aesthetic that originates in US black culture, "cool" offers resources for resistance and rebellion through access to "something better." This racialized character of "something better" – or what we can also call *jouissance* – marks black culture as both alluring and dangerous in the white imaginary.'[2]

The *jouissance*, equally
        of the 'character' on Blackstock Road

    smiling and chatting
        in beanie and fingerless   mittens

        or cussing the matchday Arsenal fans
    crowded in his pub   asking him for a chorus of   *No Woman*

                                      No Cry
        in a week that woman offered him no better

            after sixty years here than a letter   saying
    We regret   *to inform you*
            that without   *the necessary*   *documentation* …

and he was never even on that ship   the whole damn country seems to think

        he was   he flew here   in September 1957
    with his grandmother
        and a ticket they tore up at the gate

2. Shannon Winnubst, from *Way Too Cool: Selling Out Race and Ethics* (New York: Columbia University Press, 2015).

Soon Forward

My family friends were orators and preachers' sons. Pit electricians, barristers, architects and clowns. My family friends cracked jokes about the apple in your hand. *Noisy one, you got there, butt. How many decibels in that?* Grammar school kids whose time had come, my family friends taught German in their hometown comps. Made boeuf en daube and sung Bach chorales. Hung posters for Chilean Solidarity in their halls. My family friends were confident and kind. They had their stories straight, and could tell them all for Wales. A mythology gathered like mist on ridges between the Rhondda Fach and Fawr, spreading across the coalfield and the river's estuary, just never quite making it to Tiger Bay. An origins-tale of health insurance, the Revival, and high-class jobs in steel. I never thought to ask whose origins it described. Seemed obvious, and obvious how the message could be applied, beyond... our borders, beyond our voices? Beyond this telling of ourselves? What did *ourselves* look like from within? Whatever it was, I found it comforting and vivid, maybe cloying and overheard, though only in the way a child surveys a Christmas feast, with the cheeseboard half-demolished and a spoiled tablecloth, as the adults bring out brandy when he wants to just go home. But he's already home. He's always home. Because home is where he lives. My family friends knew home as they knew the harmonies for songs. And it was never quite Cardiff, never quite where I grew up. Home was somewhere less defined, both insular and epic.

Don't get me wrong, we knew of other worlds, harder worlds – worlds not wholly ours. We prayed for them, lighting candles wrapped in barbed wire, sending cards. When Mandela was released from jail we learned 'Nkosi sikelel' iAfrika', which Dad remembered from an anti-Apartheid march – and closer to home, well, we tried. Dad always stopped on Talbot St when he bumped into Ismail's dad. They talked about the cricket. One year a Kurdish man started going to our church and Mam asked him over for Sunday lunch. For starters she laid out pittas, hummus and desiccated pucks of supermarket falafel, which he hardly touched before picking at the spuds and lamb. Afterwards they helped him file his asylum claim, but it got overturned. We never heard from him again. In other words, you could say that home was as open as a door – a door you could nudge and step inside, if you knew it wasn't locked.

My family friends once asked me to recite the days of the week – for a joke, like, to see if I really was a Cardiff boy. Would my *Thursday* sound like *thirsty*, or would the *day* be round and plump? I think I failed, sounding nowhere-like, or English. I suppose that's how I sounded all the time. It made me want to follow my mates into City games, where I chanted with a zeal to make the Bob Bank proud. One day we bullied a player off the pitch – I forget his name. It was around the time that Jason Lee was getting bullied on TV, by a blackface chant comparing his hairstyle to exotic fruit. We bellowed the same chant until this other guy got subbed, pulling the knot off as he left the pitch, so his dreadlocks tumbled down. We sang till he was out of sight, to the tune of 'He's Got the Whole World in His Hands'. I can't remember who we were playing, just that I rushed home and told Dad. Then his anxious frown, his seriousness – his arm around my shoulder. *And what did you think about that? How do you think it made him feel?* I thought the guy must have felt annoyed, maybe gone back to the changing room and kicked the bath. I thought my father was telling me off, for mixing with men who smoked and swore.

But you grow out of it, don't you? You gravitate. Find the interesting, flaky boys from Welsh school, with their spray cans and spliffs down Llandaff Fields. Soon it felt like we were living everywhere – brashly, shyly, in the open, as girls slowly filtered in. Anything was possible, and the world became our home. A home not rooted now, not dusted with ancient coal. A home where you didn't have to ask permission, or worry for what you broke. We played two-toke pass and keepy-up, wore baggy jeans and rapped. We listened to Jehst on minidisc, asked Holly Morgan out. Don't get me wrong, in a way you could call it yearning. It all converged on that late-summer holiday swansong, when thirty of us hired a coach to watch Louis spit bars as MC Vinesy for the night. Sprawling on Bristol in box-fresh daps, swigging rum from Fanta cans. Somehow we all got in the club, and danced there with our half-ironic shrug – our tacky jouissance.

It made me feel sad as well as alive. It made me long for a different beat, a music only mine. I hoarded it in my lonely room, a lost historian, sketching maps of dormant sound systems, family trees of dub. I knew Kingston like the back of a book. Knew its backyards, slums, and beaches, its studio auditions. It came to me like a conversation that never seemed to finish. *Love your brothers, my friend, love your sisters.* It wasn't Bach, for a start, or Billy Bragg, not *A Festival of Folk*. My family friends wouldn't know it if it hit them with a rock. They rallied, though, when Gran died, and circled me in their mist. She was the epitome of the Rhondda, the one who made the myth make sense. She indulged me in my Cardiff ways, laughing kindly as I let her down. She did it till the week before she had her stroke. *Don't worry, lovely boy – come up sometime when you're free. Sounds like you're having fun.* At her deathbed I wasted my ten minutes with her, talking about Ellie Glynn. Gran was speechless and unconscious, but I thought that she seemed to listen. Back home I buried myself in the Congos, Alton Ellis, Phyllis Dillon...

The music spreading through me like the jingle of a rhyme.

It's only ten years later, now I'm sitting here with you – it's only now those days come back to me. We're sitting outside in the Harrow dusk, drinking with your oldest friends. Ken's flipping chicken thighs on the grill. Prosecco-flushed, Shel sprints over to the stereo, satisfying an urgent need – a need I understand – to hear Gregory Isaacs sing. *Soon forward, come turn me on yeah.*

My whiteness draws nearer, tiptoeing round the garden. Nervously at first it shows itself, or what I mean is, for the first time I can see it. It moves quickly then, on trampling heavy feet, rising through my tribute to the Cool Ruler, his chameleon career. The whiteness you know in Berkshire, which makes you feel like you're being watched. The whiteness your mother calls not being served, and I presume myself above. It leaches through these gathering synths, the echoing reverb damp, the guitars produced by Sly and Robbie back in 1979. Don't get me wrong, I mean well. I only tell you because I care. My mouth blurts *Bowie of Jamaica*, but what I mean is I'm in love.

Don't get

me

wrong.

You never have. But isn't that always the tiring thing? That you're here with me yet working to absolve our differences. Stroking my arm, too patiently, as though asking me to stop, till the whiteness that feels at home in speech falls quiet in your hand. It's the familiar tiring story, unfolding subtly each time – one of ownership confused with care, desire with understanding. But if I could only pay attention, only listen to this song, there's a chance I could hear its deeper groove, the rhythm of its thinking. The vocal, the guitar, the dubplate: the progression towards silence. How each component contributes, while the space around it heightens.

Toasting for Pronouns

You doesn't always mean *you*, you know.
U-Roy ≠ Yabby You.
U-Roy > Yabby You? Debatable, but surely
Big Youth beats anything you got.
N.B. His I-and-I
does *not* apply
to you, by which I mean, in this case,
me. Sister Nancy
she a one in a three million
the only woman DJ with degree
but Yellowman could be my favourite,
lothario stood six feet tall, cavorting
obliquely onstage in Riverside
when last I saw him.
Zungguzungguguzungguzeng…
Babylon a use dem brain.
Babylon is *wily,* encompassing both
tyrannous singularity and plural force.
The lyric 'I' doesn't always refer to I
though sometimes, and mostly here, it does.
I'm Count Machuki firing up 'More Scorcha'
for the Down Beat crew, on a crackling night in June.
I'm too scared ever to travel where
my heroes ruled the dance.
I'm worried I won't be welcome there
though whenever I listen to him
the lyric I-Roy doesn't seem –
could *never* seem –
to care.

Party Time

Memory now go forward, one last time. Memory
now settle, in the place where we can finish this,
right at the moment when the Bildungsroman flops
exhausted, on the other side of innocence. A Bristol
wine bar, Tuesday night. First term at university,

still two years out from knowing you, so for now I'm
hopeless still, and homesick, and singularly failing
to convert my encyclopaedic theories about lover's rock
into practice. But hey, at least here people seem to know
that dancing works best when the music's tight

and the Reggae Soc session is proving it tonight,
bringing jam after jam to the heaving floor. Decades
zigzag and congeal. Dynasties of soundclash titans,
studio shamans, falsettos and backing bands
converge upon this dubious telos, as we appropriate

and skank. *I love to see my people living in love,*
I hate to see them fighting or swimming in blood.
From a distance you could say that there's a beauty
in our gurning, or is it a forgetting, as when a girl
with a nose ring and light-blonde dreads

draws the moment into herself, eyes closed, and mouths
the lyrics to a Heptones song she briefly owns. What a
palaver. What a mash up. What a bam-bam. We're a type
of coded euphemism that both flatters and offends.
History entrenches, like a garrison, round the speaker,

and never with its lines straight, or its ethics. Never without
an angle that feeds directly onto trauma, as my favourite ever
vocalist could tell you. It's 1973. Slim Smith wanders
the Kingston streets, bewildered and alone. Discharged
from Bellevue Asylum, the 'famously troubled singer'

tries to break into his home. Glass shatters. It lacerates
his arms. He tumbles to the floor and bleeds, unaided,
to a coma. He passes there, into tragedy, into connoisseurship,
into rumour, then disappears until a sample finds him in the blue
somehow possessive light of a port city at midnight.

III

Nothing looks satisfied,
but there is no real reason to move on much further:
this isn't a bad place;
why not pretend

we wished for it?

Jorie Graham, 'Over and Over Stitch'

September's Child

Hormonally it ripens, tickling the blood, building
through the part of me that would be womb,

a premonition of loss or change, an over-fattened moon.
Saccharine and festive, it makes of me a boy in bed

failing to sleep on his birthday eve. Still I find myself
September's child, bookish, mild, ever eldest in the year,

a connoisseur of subtle treats, like ravioli from the tin,
the adult jokes in Asterix, or better yet a malady

that softly lowers you to the settee but doesn't stop
your eyes from lapping at a page. Every year,

sure as morning bell, I'd feel the bulge descend upon
my tonsil gland, as now I feel the blossoming

of an earthier and urgent need, a waft of chestnut
smoke at summer's end. I don't know what it is,

I only know it comes in August with a sky of school-
sweater grey and declining light. My pinky custard

shivers, barely set within its rabbit mould. Sometimes
it only takes a bar of Charles Trenet unwinding through

'La Mer' and I'm awash. A salt of yearning rises
to my throat. Everywhere I look the children are

younger, or else I'm fatter and forgetful, still stumbling
on the brink of coming into something long deserved.

Wards

oh let me have been born to this – forever – the visiting hour extending –
as I pace the building reading certain signs – anonymous and queasy – let
me count on every kindness – sidestep empty trolleys – riding lifts to wings
named after dreadful words – nephrology – where wires link to sockets –
that describe a pact – I'd call it one of guardianship – or power – pyjama
tops unbuttoned by hand – that swabs your chest because – it's needed
– just how often can you say that – let me rest awhile – attention tapered
to a bedside – paper opened on a crossword – that prolongs the not quite
knowing – how does one empower a guardian – the coffee machine is
broken – but it can't be right – that I feel safe inside this warren – its
corridors unscrolling – like small print in a contract being – always not
quite broken – let the night be still attended – not rented or applauded –
the monitor still pulsing green – let someone else be born

Post-Historical Teatime

blue-green dapple of the cul-de-sac
gold antipodean sun   it dazzles
like a promise of untrammelled growth
the saturated screen   *neighbours*
everybody needs   a lounger ruby
on the pool   but more than that
the colour that I wish to fix is silver
aluminium silver of the coke cans
stocked by Ben's mam in her fridge
those babies really washed down
ideology's demise   let's not say

that we were idiots   we were children
making guesses off the world that
we could see   it tasted good and had
no calories   the jingle made us laugh
neighbours   neighbours   kind of
comforting when whistled and a little
understanding seemed the least you
could expect   a politics could grow

from that like walking back from school
I held Ben's discman and we took one
headphone each   until an afternoon
Liam yanked them off and told us
how some nutter nuked America
while we were still in period 6
and so the telly all that evening was
a plane and then   the flames
I don't remember when the loop
was cut or service was resumed
but next day things   were different
all the colours seemed to drain

American Gratitude

for Brandon Kreitler

Stuck in line, the absent subject strays
in monogrammed splendour
past the border guard who yanks
him back and strips him down,
confiscating his appliances. He's
only obeying orders, his brisk
sincerity a pose internalised
on training day, or learned
through the longer reifications
of a nation determining
its manner. The subject flagged
on his software and gets taken
to one side for secondary
questioning. This parable
unfolds in parallel to the beloved
and unobtainable landscape
beyond the window, which infuses
the subject with a sense of safety
and excitement, even as he waits
to explain his overwrought predicament
in private to another guard.

I've never mastered
the American gesture,
how often or intensely
to make your gratitude known
to those who wait on you,
how that trivial but vital thanks
should be distinguished from the love
you bear for those who owe you
nothing, yet surpass the modest grace
a friendship might require.
In either case appreciation
seems to interrupt an ethic
of tacit service.

From the bookie-counter window,
which has narrowed to his only
aching border, the subject is released
to enter the nearly forbidden land
of unmeasured measures and federal
charm – a tipping culture
he's already forgotten
how to satisfy.

New York Morning, Six Years On

The manhole on 53rd snorts a bower of steam
around the tilted couple smooching through a shameless PDA

that's got the cabbies honking wedding marches,
tugging on their horns. Have I succeeded so far

in having you on? That *poem of place* you thought I'd botched
is coming back for season two, as a classier brand of porn.

Allow me to mansplain. On arrival in New York you'll note
the pace of life that turns routine commutes into a high

stakes hockey match. I learned this to my cost, all over
again this rush hour morn, as I held my hot drip close

and nibbled my muffin, snug beneath a tech bro's arm,
an obtrusive foreign dork. *Hey, buddy – hey, how about a knife*

and fork? I could've sworn I heard him quip. I was dashing
to MoMA to meet my friend for her law firm's yearly perk,

where they open the doors two hours before the schmucks
pile in to gawp. Ambulating lordly through the empty gallery

I only rued the way they'd moved Picasso's *Demoiselles*
to a corner where, if you didn't know, you could've missed

those groovy belles. Otherwise I had a blast. My friend left
at 9 for work, and with an hour still left before the hordes

I caught the Rauschenberg. To think the last time I was here
I was clueless to his shtick; to think I thought New York would gift

its secrets to me, a hick. A wide-eyed rube, an ingénue, a limey
flaneur prick. I blush through Bob's Black Mountain years

and hit the Fulton room. A pile of trash and bric-a-brac,
it instructs me what to say: *No taste / No object / No idea.* I'm more

than six years late. His buddy Cage still sounds a scream
and *he's* sixty years in date. The infinite postmodern wince,

the cabinets of crap. The world we just appropriate,
the passé-ness of that. They're dancing but not dancing

strapped with chairs across their backs. The paintings sprout with grit
and shirts and taxidermy gags. I'm rushing through, I need the loo,

I'm airless and bereft. I'm doomed to lust for coloured silks,
for the little meaning left. My syntax is ripped and pathetically fixed,

I've nothing to offer you, Bobby. You didn't catch my first book
but you'd think it so twee and sloppy. I sang the song of avenues

you captured with a tyre track. I had sleepless nights over mixed
reviews that patiently listed my drawbacks. Hyperventilating,

caked in mud, I sprint through the last installations,
and run out then left and collapse on Fifth, where Trump

Tower grins through the morning. Bathed in a glancing
plutocrat sun, I feel like I'll never stop falling. The city

swarms over me, crackle and dirt, a pitiless grinding signal.
It doesn't love me or help me up. It pulps me to beef on its griddle.

Sun Has Spoken

Visible over the mountain
  a cloud
    blurs soft and thin against the farther sky,
        a javelin thrown flat to pierce
            a heart at speed
     but with all the vigour
    drained most gently from its arc.

I felt luckier when the sky
    called wantonly for me
      to gorge on it, happier
    now it bathes me
      in an equal light.

It is afternoon or
    evening. I read or watch the twitching
     shrubs, or cradle my tumbler of local beer,
    meniscus
       wobbling in time.

Whichever way, the sun
    has spoken, and the hay
  is almost baled for autumn.
      (I am in a place
    for making hay,
        it's true.)

Tonight will be a night
    of unsurpassable grief
        for someone,
     a night I will pass through
    clinging fast
  to my protections,
    knowing well the wind

  will nag until they rend apart –
    that the mountain is lunar
      and brutally silver when the sun
             goes down,
    rescinding its unlikely vow
     that we are loved, and known.

Poem in which my hairline recedes

and Mary's dress tears   past all stitching
in the screen door warping shut   forever
Roy Orbison croons in memory   of the follicles
too mischievous or weak   to stay with me   a torch song
no less passionate   for being foolish   and I'm scared
both at the grand banality   of knowing I ain't that
young any more   and at what would happen   if she met me
Mary   this far down the road   as yet unable to offer her
a ride   It's a slow-burn mortification   a debt being bled from me
instalment by invisible   instalment   while my hairdresser
ventures kindly jokes   and lathers my endangered locks
with coconut shampoo   Her laughter   confiscates the dream
of late nights without consequence   of the songs I wrote
in my attic room   when I was 17   Springsteen was only 25
when he wrote   *Born to Run*   his album of awakening and fear
at the chances hurtling past   on the irretrievable highway
Christ   I can't   stop staring   at those deathless gatefold shots
where leather-jacketed he beams   and leans on Clarence
man cleavage and medallion   on show   his hair a black
hydrangea   sprouting to eternity   I want to run   my fingers
like wind   through the rolled-down window   to the roots
and hold him   with his harmonica   as he sings to Mary
and explains   how they've got   *one last chance to*
make it real   knowing there's no chance   in hell
that chance could pass them by

Shopping with Mam

Panini await, and half-price coats. Happy
to help, she takes my arm and sails us, double-
masted, into town. Nye points the way, stroppy
on his plinth, unsure of how his struggle

led to menswear, level two. Socialism in one
family! She does justice where she can, finding clothes
to redistribute from the shop-front mannequins.
Assistants don't know whom to schmooze,

the buyer or the bought-for, don't know who's
upholding whom. My welfare state, my bail-
out, she who keeps me in tidy shoes –
I kiss her with the shyness of a holy fool

suffered to be idle in God's love. Her love
is chivalry profound. She wishes me nice things,
gives me roses by the armful with my daily loaf
of bread. I look away as she keys her PIN.

Obsolete Heartbreak Suite

Lacking love, I found love
in an empty ballroom filled

with voices: voices of women
singing songs that men had tricked

in sadness. Flugelhorns and pizzicato strings.
A tone always resolving in the sense

of having cried. Heartbreak tasted
chemical, like lipstick accidentally

taken in my mouth, drawn carelessly
in the mirror where I saw myself disguised

as what I wanted badly, wanting me.

       Wishin' and hopin' and thinkin' and prayin'…

The jukebox so obliging, so reliable
in its taste. For old time's sake, I linger

there tonight, feeding coin after coin
into the rusted slot. This one for

the splendour of a drum, that made
the world feel like my belly at a ten-

foot drop. This one for the moonlit
nothing of a dancefloor, each night I

swayed unsteadily, alone. I wanted love
like someone waiting on an answer, or

news that brings blood crowding to your
ears. The flood held back, the hissing,

all that pressure going nowhere, and
meanwhile songs of boyfriends, chiffon

rustling in the dark. They sound thin
tonight, and haunted. They're dancing

somewhere different. But I'm trying to
feel their trick again – to win their love.

Doggies

Seeing you snuggled first thing in the basket of our sofa
as your waking slowly spreads through you and shakes the fog,
I know before the water hits my instant coffee
there are richer ways to live, but none to love.

You amble to me, wrapped imperially in the toga
of your purple blanket, scrawled with stray and glinting hair,
and kiss me as I measure out three spoons of yoghurt
for the boring breakfast that I eat to stay alive

for as long as this unravelled world will let us,
where the land is hoarded far beyond our means,
for as long as we're still crowded out of windowsills and pensions
and you play with strangers' collies on the street,

for as long as there's a world with half the kindness
that you bring to it with every thankless task and thought,
for as long as there are versions of this morning
with you sipping from a mug whose golden pooch

playing on the curving surface of its china
is an emblem of the heart you hold secure
through every setback, every time I feel a failure
and drag down on the ballast of your love.

I need for you to know as we both stumble over 30
that there's nothing you could long for that I don't,
and though there's something sickly, something silly in the patois
that we age into and speak when we're alone

I tell you now there's only ever glory in your yearning
to be woken by a scamper, to a ruffle in our bed.
I can't pretend to swear to you we'll ever have a garden
but stick with me, I promise, and you'll always have your dog.

Benevolence Test

At Tito's Mausoleum, I finally asked the world
        if it was good. The complex held a vista
of the tramways, crumbling roofs and tower blocks
        of Novi Grad, and Tito's medals lay in state
on velvet cushions next to photographs of Tito
        waving as he disembarked from private planes
accompanied by leaders of the Non-Alignment Pact.
        Can anyone say they're non-aligned?
My throat tingled fitfully but not enough to change
        our plans. The manager at our hostel
swore her country looked back fondly
        on the days when Tito ruled. They were harder
but simpler, and there was work. Ask world
        if it employs us, on any sort of terms.

Back home I succumbed, I sickened –
        a hyperinflation raged along my overstretched
dependencies. At a pharmacy counter I handed
        my prescription slip to be redeemed
for plastic-coated capsules, bitter on the tongue:
        I swallowed in our kitchen as resistance built
deep in the code of my pampered cells.
        Ask world why my cells in particular.
Ask safety net instead of cure to cheat
        a death I don't believe in.

Recovery occurred. Perhaps it was linked obscurely
        to the light pollution seeping through
the blinds. I slept here on the sofa, through a winter,
        whenever I snored, under the watch of invitations
to friends' weddings. We hung them as decorations
        or reminders, to mark the days, though fluctuations
in the oil stock never threatened the sign outside.
        It broadcast a continual thought
of pizza, neon through the night, a resolution crumbling
        in the realism of the street. One night,
very early, unable now to sleep, I bought
        tickets through a price comparison site –
the algorithm lost, or maybe won, but so did I,

making good at last on a promise to attend
my partner's cousin's wedding. Ask love if it can heal
        the distances it travels, through long
but intermittent rain. Ask hospitality to extend
        beyond the borders love inhabits.

A model for democracy: the airport
        in an emirate, as it ferries its wanderers
from gate to gate. People need to fly
        and they're assisted; property is tagged
and tracked, in case of misadventure.
        Will the law uphold us half as carefully
beyond the exits? Two thousand of us surging
        through this omnidirectional moment,
obeying in perfect freedom the procedures
        of safe passage. Two hundred of us detaching
for each onward flight, four of us in excitement
        for a family reunion. The greater we, the lesser,
universal embrace or nuclear wall: a pronoun
        that never seems to capture
the phenomenon it longs to. We're transferring
        to Mumbai, for a reception serving
dim sum on the roof, a terrace backed against
        a tenement, where the bride's side
waits to meet. Ask world to stay invisible.
        Ask violence to split from gain:
please cheap without deep-drilling,
        please remittance but no commission.

In the nowhere land between security and flight,
        on a travellator scrolling past dissolved
and reassembled ads, I linger in their suggestion
        of technocratic good. Is it what I wanted? Is it good
like how I dreamed? Count me as one who'd sooner be
        forgiven than correct. Red, white and black
shine the logos of my bank. A fisherman sets sail
        through misted air, for a Confucian tableau
just around the river bend. My bank invests in water,
        in the clean water of his river, and the banyans
working roots beneath the engineered soil. Ask world
        if propaganda. Ask rising tides if world.

Ask melting waterfront to hold until the terrace
　　　　opens to amazing smog, a florescent polis
labouring through the night, where in 1534 a viceroy
　　　　claimed treaty of possession. Now Amit who
works in start-up tech says world is getting safer,
　　　　says wealth is spreading further, and his father's
the new owner of an NBA franchise.
　　　　Ask which of us is wishful. Ask why am I not sure
as the test proves inconclusive and the floodlights
　　　　press their bright results against a wilderness of cloud.

The Mercury Mine

after Dylan

For anything so thin and wild there must be
graft: long shifts crouching in the seam
at the delicate joint where rock could give
and gush the silver that your genius conspired
to hide. What, you thought this was any old
everyday pact with brilliance – bread delivered
hot and easy from the devil's van? Nice dream
bakery you got there, pal. Meanwhile the elevator's
dropping storeys through the pit, carrying the few
who know that mercury's a hard and dirty trove,
a supper you gotta sing for first, and sing for,
groping – sing for while the blisters needle
hot and weeping on your picking hand.

Take 12. Fragment. False start. Remake.
*When you're lost in Juarez, raining, and it's
Easter too*, and there's nothing left to do
but hack the syllable till it wedges tight
and *you're lost in the rain in Juarez and it's
Eastertime too*, with a gravity that drops
then fails, the smell of another country's
road and liquor fogging heavy in your mind,
you'll know then that you've found the place
I mean, the deepest shaft, where you must
go to work, however much you stoop
and hurt, and dig until you strike upon
that metal burning liquid in your palm.

Pink Cones

The door will open to a different garden,
air more intimate and careful in its reach.
A leg that fell asleep, hooked under me
on the lawn, buckles as it wakes, becoming
mine again. The songs will be unbanished
in your throat, riddling clouds of midges
make their answer known. Sun so hot
I'm slapped with it gleams mellow on
a leaf, now the old king and his henchmen
quit the throne. I hear they just grew
tired of it, the killing and denial, so they're
living free and righteous in a wood.
And wouldn't you? Can't we? Permission
sizzles on our arms. The cows will be
unbanished and the stones; all the people
making gallows turned to glaziers and clowns.
In the morning of the chestnuts we will
ride the timid horses, while flowers keep
the records, we shall know their names.

These ones, especially, I could almost place –
frothing in the treetops, half a dozen
to a branch. Pink cones, strawberry
against the green, swaying in their clusters,
unsupported, reaching up. So much escapes
the telling and yet the angles still refresh –
the festival commencing at a different height.
The paths will be unbanished as my feet,
still tingling, return along the loop, to meet
you at the pavilion, my courier to spring.

Notes and Acknowledgements

Thanks to the editors of the following journals, websites, and anthologies where these poems first appeared, sometimes in different versions: *Cold Fire: Poetry Inspired by David Bowie* (The Rialto, 2017), *Disclaimer, Islands Are But Mountains: New Poetry from the United Kingdom* (Platypus Press, 2019), the *London Review Bookshop* blog, *The Lonely Crowd, Prac Crit, Poems in Which, Poetry Birmingham Literary Journal, Poetry Spotlight, Poetry Wales, Where the Birds Sing Our Names* (Seren, 2021), and *The White Review*.

'Doxology':

> *Praise God from whom all blessings flow*
> *Praise Him all creatures here below*
> *Praise Him above, ye heavenly host*
> *Praise Father, Son and Holy Ghost*

'Poem on 27th Birthday':

> *Cuore Kaka. Milan è casa mia.*

> 'The Heart of Kaka. Milan is my home.'

'Real Rain':

> 'Someday a real rain will come and wash all this scum off the streets.' – Travis Bickle, *Taxi Driver*

I wrote this poem for an event at the Betsey Trotwood, organised by Jon Stone, Kate Potts, and Holly Hopkins, titled 'An A-Z of Villains'.

'Karaoke King':

> *Paham mae dicter, O Myfanwy,*
> *Yn llenwi'th lygaid duon di?*

> 'Why so the anger, oh Myfanwy,
> That fills your dark eyes?'

'Ubi Caritas':

Ubi caritas et amor, Deus ibi est.

'Where there is tender love and care, God is present.'

I'm deeply indebted to the many careful readers that the poems in this book have had over the years. Thanks in particular to: Zoë Brigley, John Clegg, Joey Connolly, Emily Hasler, Oli Hazzard, Holly Hopkins, Sarah Howe, Rowena Knight, Melissa Lee-Houghton, Alex MacDonald, John McCollough, Kate Potts, Vidyan Ravinthiran, Martha Sprackland, Jon Stone, Chrissy Williams, Alison Winch, and Jane Yeh. Thanks to John Canfield and Alex Bell, whose excellent 'Bowieoke' and 'Dylanoke' nights, also at the Betsey Trotwood, furnished poems in the book.

Thanks to my editor at Seren, Amy Wack, for her patience and support. Thanks to Irene Baldoni and all the team at Georgina Capel Associates.

Thanks as always to my parents, Phil and Ceri George; my sisters, Catrin and Hannah George; my grandmother, Mary Davies; and Reena and Peter Keeble. My grandfather, Gordon Davies, died during the writing of this book, and 'God Willing' is dedicated to his memory. The book itself is dedicated to Jasmin Kapur Keeble, whom I love very much. May it one day be a dog instead.

A note on 'A History of Jamaican Music'

An extract from an earlier version of this sequence was published in *Poetry Wales*, alongside a note discussing the genesis of the project, and I would like to thank Nia Davies for valuable dialogue in the run-up to publication. I would like to repeat my thanks to Zoë Brigley for her feedback on this poem in particular, at a formative moment in its composition.

Aside from the works credited in-text, I would like to acknowledge Steve Barrow and Peter Dalton's seminal *The Rough Guide to Reggae* (London: Penguin, 2004) and two articles from the *Jamaican Observer*, which provided valuable background information (and ideas) for particular poems in the sequence: 'Slim Smith, the influential singer' (Friday, August 17, 2012) and 'When Norman Manley won and lost a referendum' by Lance Neita (Sunday, July 27, 2014). 'The Night (Dub)' intersperses lines from 'Nicodemus' by The Congos with 'The Night' by Henry Vaughan, another great poetic telling of the story in John 3: 1-21.

Below is a list of tracks that offer up quotations or allusions through the sequence. Should the reader be inclined, they would make a pretty great (and roughly chronological) playlist.

Lord Laro – 'Jamaican Referendum Calypso'
The Ethiopians – 'Train to Skaville'
The Skatalites – 'Guns of Navarone'
The Uniques – 'People Rocksteady'
Alton Ellis – 'Rocksteady'
Derrick Harriott – 'The Loser'
The Paragons – 'On the Beach'
The Techniques – 'Love Is Not a Gamble'
Lee 'Scratch' Perry – 'Croaking Lizard'
The Congos – 'Nicodemus'
Bob Marley & the Wailers – 'No Woman, No Cry'
The Uniques – 'My Conversation'
Gregory Isaacs – 'Soon Forward'
Sister Nancy – 'Only Woman DJ with Degree'
Yellowman – 'Zungguzungguguzungguzeng'
Sizzla – 'Babylon A Use Dem Brain'
Count Machuki – 'More Scorcha'
The Heptones – 'Party Time'
I-Wayne – 'Living in Love'
The Maytals / Sister Nancy – 'Bam Bam'

Thanks to all musicians, vocalists, producers, deejays, and reggae fans who have written, performed, and spread the word about these songs down the years, providing untold joy and inspiration.